Understanding

The Body

Language

ISBN 978-1-304-78012-6
Copyright 2014   All Rights Reserved.

First Edition

"The body constantly informs us what is wrong with our bodies. It has its own language. Our interpretation may be wrong but the body is always right! We need to learn how to 'Understand the Body Language!'" – Ed Portley Jr

"It is the unseen and the spiritual in people that determines the outward and the actual." - Thomas Carlyle

Prologue

"What is wrong with me? Why do I feel this way? How am I hurting and I don't even know what I did to myself?"

Do you find yourself saying things like this? If not, **this book is not for you.**

This book is for people who:
- Are in pain, whether it is chronic or acute
- Think they have an old injury that still hurts
- Is susceptible to mosquito bites
- Truly want to know the cause of their condition
- Want to be out of pain forever

I went to massage school and learned a lot about energy; how it flows, what causes stagnation and how it affects the body. I learned Reflexology, Chinese Medicine and the Hindu Chakra energy system. All three believe their individual systems work to help people feel better and be healthier.

So I thought "If they each truly work, then they must work together in a magnificent way.

And that they do!

In this book I will show you the ROOT CAUSE that is causing your condition. You may want to know why you have a particular medical condition, skin problem or a malady involving the nervous system. Here are some examples:

People who have low back pain are afraid they won't be able to provide for their family, those with money issues. They are afraid they won't be able to pay the mortgage, car payment, utility bills and/or have enough money to buy food for the family. These won't be single individuals but people with a child, children or some other person dependent on them for food, clothing and shelter, the basic needs for survival.

Ok, so you read that and thought "In this economy, who DOESN"T worry about having enough money?" This is true. But the worry or fear affects everyone differently. Some aren't bothered by it, others get low back pain and some get tight neck muscles.

Let's do another condition.

I had just finished a massage with a client who is a chiropractor. He said he wanted to show me a technique that he uses in his practice. He said for me to find a tight muscle that was bothering me. So I said it was my neck muscles. He had me do certain things, he said some phrases and, without massaging my muscles, without touching them, he was able to relax them.

He used an energy technique called NET, Neuro-Emotional Technique. It is a fascinating technique that gets to the core issue of the problem. The only issue for me was that one needed to be considered a health care provider who had the credentials to diagnose conditions. As a massage therapist, I don't have those credentials.

About a year went by when I came across a website by a massage therapist who highly recommended a technique called EFT, Emotional Freedom Technique.

The more I read about it, the more I fell in love with it.

EFT was founded by Gary Craig, a Stanford Engineer, circa 1995 in California. You can find his official website at www.Emofree.com.

Preface

This book will describe what I have come to know as the truth as to how the body works. It is my own theory, based on my knowledge and experiences. All will not agree with me, and that's ok. We are all entitled to our opinions. I thank you for being interested in my opinion and wanting to know more.

Throughout my career as a massage therapist and as a massage therapy instructor, I have learned many things about the human body. The human body is amazing. I have found that the body is, in its entirety, energy! I have found that the body, being energy, has the ability to heal itself. If someone were to say that I am a healer, I would disagree. I would describe myself as a facilitator in the healing process, guiding the body to heal itself. Or, to better understand what I mean, I would describe myself as a flute. A flute makes no noise; it is the wind going through the flute that makes the noise. I am the flute, while the energy is the wind. I allow the energy to flow through me, and not by me.

The purpose of writing this book is to help others realize the healing power of the body and to bring awareness how the body informs us of the cause of the maladies in which we suffer. I believe that negative emotions, thoughts, beliefs, feelings and ideas create and cause all physical problems, maladies, dis-eases, pain, dysfunctions, malfunctions, etc.

I will take the reader through the process of identifying the problem or weakness of the body, determining the cause and the solution to the problem. To do that, I need to teach the readers of the Chakras (Hindu) and the Meridians (Chinese and Japanese), each describing the energy of the body. Understanding these systems will be the foundation of determining the emotion behind the disease, sickness, condition or malady.

I will teach the reader how to stimulate the meridians in an attempt to realign the energy flow. This will be the technique used to break away the connection of the body to the emotions. By emotions, I am referring also to each individual's belief systems. Once identification is made, the healing technique is quite simple.

It is my hope that the information in this book inspires the reader to find the cause of his/her condition(s) and can overcome them. I believe this is a possible accomplishment for those following the guidelines and suggestions.

I will suggest, as you come to the sections on emotions and their relationship to the chakras and meridians, consider your own ailments and see for yourself if you believe any of these emotions to be true in your life and the thoughts that go through your mind.

There will be certain assumptions that will be made regarding the use of the material and information in this book. One fundamental assumption will be recognition of the theory that "the outward is an expression of the inward", that emotions can and do cause physical problems. The other assumption would be that the body could heal itself if given the opportunity.

The most important assumption that will be made by me throughout this book is

NEGATIVE EMOTIONS CAUSE ALL BODILY AILMENTS, CONDITIONS AND DISEASES!

This is not the belief of traditional western medicine. It is not my intent to lead anyone astray from their doctors, medications or western medicine. It is a theory that I hope is investigated by doctors, surgeons and scientists to help bring about a quality of health and life for every human being.

If it is your intent to read another person's body, my suggestion is to keep confidential any information discerned, use only with the higher good in mind, don't use any of this information in a negative way against anyone and acquire written permission prior to disclosing any personal information!

Lastly, there are two books which I recommend you read that will help you understand energy and the body if, for some reason, this book fails to explain it adequately or if it fails to provide you with the answers you are searching for. One book is called "Feelings Buried Alive Never Die"

By Karol K. Truman. The other book is called "Heal Your Body" by Louise Hay.

These two books are quite similar in nature. They describe in detail how the energy system in the body works. There is information in these books that, when added to my book, will give you a comprehensive understanding of how emotions cause physical abnormalities, diseases and medical conditions. They will describe how negative energy is held in the body and what diseases are associated with specific emotions.

It is my hope that you find the origin of whatever it is you are searching for. I hope you come to realize the emotions that are causing problems in you and how to help you return to a healthy state.

Please enjoy the book!

Chapter One

Our Body as Energy

So, what do I mean by our emotions cause all bodily ailments, conditions and diseases? When we look at ourselves, we generally see a figure with a particular color shirt, matching pants and a hairstyle. Perhaps we see someone's fashion sense, or lack thereof. Or we notice other accessories that have a glitter or shine to them.

Some people have the ability to recognize certain emotions on a person's face. It has been said that the outward is an expression of the inward, what happens above, so below. What happens on the physical plane also happens on the spiritual plane, and vice versa. "They" also say that the eyes are a mirror to your soul. Just as the color yellow can indicate jaundice and blue lips can indicate lack of oxygen supply, so too can the body give us clues as to what is happening inside, what emotions we are experiencing.

For example, one might expect to see a red face on someone who seems extremely happy or excited. Or a red face could indicate someone is mad or angry and his or her blood pressure might be raised.

What we don't see sometimes is more important than what we do see. What we don't see is the energy that allows our bodies to have this reaction. What we don't see is the entire picture in order to determine what causes the problems with our bodies.

The first thing we need to realize is that we are energetic beings. We ARE energy. A skeptic may say "how do you know we are energy, was it ever proven?" Oh yes, it HAS been proven scientifically. Scientists have been able to determine that inside our cells we have a nucleus. Inside the nucleus we have atoms. And atoms are units of energy made from electrons, protons and neutrons. I often liken atoms to the makeup of a simple electrical wire. An electrical wire has a red, a black and a green wire, a positive, a negative and a ground (neutral).

There are billions and billions of cells in the body and each cell has many atoms. This means there are more atoms than we can count in the human body.

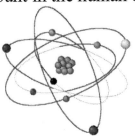

Albert Einstein also proved the existence of energy. He said that Energy Equals Mass Times the Speed of Light Squared $(E=MC)^2$. In our nerves, it has been proven that the speed of energy, the speed of nerve transmission, can range from 250 to 350 feet per second.

I believe the body can heal itself. Doctors and medicine can and do assist the body in its attempt to heal itself. I believe that whenever possible, we should try alternative therapies, especially the therapies that have been proven to be effective in clearing up any abnormalities. It has been shown in some traditional healing methods that the stagnation or decreased flow of energy can and will cause problems in the muscles, organs and tissues in any particular area.

Energy is supposed to flow with a constant movement with a nice even flow. When energy doesn't flow in a particular area of the body, we will manifest problems in the area of that stagnation. Stagnant energy must be released from the body!! I cannot stress this most important fact enough. When we "hold something in", it is the energy that is being held. If we don't release it, it will come out on its own. We don't want that. It's not good if it comes out on its own. It will come out in various ways. It may come out as a disease, a rash, as a pimple or even a wart. It may be released as cancer, or some other type of lesion or cyst. The possibilities are endless.

Let's take a look at a simple pimple or acne. I want you to look at it for a minute as a volcano. What exactly is a volcano? A volcano is the surface of the earth (skin), which has a lot of heat deep to the surface (energy), and an extremely hot (hotter than the surrounding area) liquid substance (puss) below the surface. When the energy builds up enough pressure under the surface, the volcano will "blow its top". And so does the pimple. It gets a black head and when it discharges the puss, it has released its pressure, and the pressure is its energy.

There are many different beliefs and traditions that describe the way energy exists and flows in the body. Three major traditions include reflexology, Asian Bodywork Therapy and the Hindu chakra system. There is one commonality that exists amongst these traditions. It is the flow of the energy. It must flow smoothly in order to obtain optimal health. If the flow of the energy decreases or becomes stagnant, the corresponding organs will not have enough to operate significantly and will manifest problems, complications or disease. Maintaining the flow of energy is vital to the health of the body.

Often times, when I am attempting to determine what may be wrong with a client, I utilize these traditions. If I don't get an answer from one, I will look to another for the answer. Or I will tell the story by combining the characteristics and emotions of all three traditions. I use my intuition to help me decide which I think is the correct scenario. I have over a 95% success rate of being correct. The remaining percentage is generally the ones that I find that are reluctant to believe, the skeptical, the closed minded. At times, I find that the person who has a physical condition yet the emotions that are causing these problems are not ones that the individual experiences. In such cases, these people are empaths, that is, they soak up other people's negative energies. Remember when your mother said "Put yourself in their shoes, how would YOU feel if that happened to you". Or maybe you have heard the saying "walk a mile in someone's shoes". When we do this we do actually create and experience that energy and it can cause the physical conditions of that energy.

As stated in the preface, I believe that some type of emotion causes all physical complaints. I hope to be able to adequately explain my beliefs regarding this in this book.

Chapter Two

The Emotions and Beliefs

Our emotions and beliefs are what make each of us individual and unique. Included in this category are our deeds and our habits. As we grow, the people that we live with, the situations we experience and the thoughts in our heads all contribute to the total outcome of whom we are, what we are about and how we live life. They say it "takes a village to raise a child". And that is so true. Every single person that comes into our lives influences us in some way. We will change our way of thinking just because we have met them, listened to their experiences and decide whether or not to believe the same thing.

Our emotions and beliefs control our bodies. It is the driving force for who we are to become. They control our health, way of life, our experiences and our relationships with other people.

Our deeds are the physical manifestation of our thoughts, beliefs, ideas and emotions. If we think or believe that a weaker person is someone who we should help, perhaps by standing up for him or her, that's what we do. However, if we think or believe a weaker person is someone who we can manipulate, we may try to sell him or her something they may not need or have any use for. There may be some who think a weaker person is someone who should learn how to be stronger. Maybe that motivates them to open a karate studio. There can be so many possibilities for each and every scenario based on each and every individual's beliefs and thoughts.

Our habits are formed by the thoughts and beliefs of how we should behave, how we should dress, how we should live or even what we should do and in what order we should do it in.

Some people have a routine. A routine is a habit of doing things in a particular order. The way we start a habit is to first, believe we need to do something, or want to do something. It is the acknowledgement of the outcome. It is the accomplishment that is desired. Presumably, it is something we enjoy. If we enjoy doing it, we want to do it over and over again. That's what makes us do things habitually.

Psychologists say that the first 21 days of trying to make something a habit, or breaking a habit, is the hardest barrier to overcome. But once overcome, the new habit is formed. They say that after 90 days that habit has been instilled into every cell of our body. The first 21 days are the hardest but when you reach 90 days, you have created a new habit. And so the cycle is renewed with the new thought, idea or belief.

Our beliefs are just as important as emotions in the cause of physical conditions or maladies. These are the writings on the walls of our minds. I'll give an example. While growing up, maybe your parents said to you "there are children in poor countries who don't have anything to eat, so eat all of your food". Remember how proud your mother was when you finished all your food? After hearing this repeatedly, one may come to the conclusion that they must finish all the food on their plate. This thought stays with us for the rest of our life. Thus, we tend to overeat.

As a teen growing up in Philadelphia, a blue collar city, I was a "growing boy". I felt like I had to eat more because of it. I heard things like "you can't be full, eat some more" and "are you going to make me throw away all this food?"

We don't like to waste food or maybe we won't save the leftovers because there isn't enough for an entire meal, and so we over-eat.

Restaurants tend to give you much more food than a nutritional serving, and so when eating out, we tend to over eat. We also want a lot for our money, and the portions tend to be large. Again, we won't eat the leftovers. It's as if we still have the desire to please our parents by finishing all the food.

It may seem like I'm rambling but this type of conversation happens to everyone. Maybe the topic is changed a bit, but the idea is the same.

There are many emotions that someone could be experiencing. For example, if someone is experiencing grief, sorrow, sadness or depression you will find this emotion sits in the lungs if the sadness is female related or in the large intestine if it is male related. It also shows up in the arms, bronchial tubes, and nose and in the skin. It can show up as eczema, psoriasis, asthma, scleroderma, fibromyalgia and more.

Timing is essential in determining the specific emotion that is causing a particular problem. Many diseases have what is called an "incubation period". This is the time starting with the first point of contact with an agent to the time when a condition, disease or problem manifests itself. Many physical problems show up within hours or days of an emotionally traumatic event. When determining the emotional cause, start with the approximate day or date that a problem showed up. Then figure out the location of the physical problem, then the emotions that are involved.

We will cover a few case studies to show you how to determine the cause of your own physical complaints.

Chapter Three

The Nervous and Endocrine System

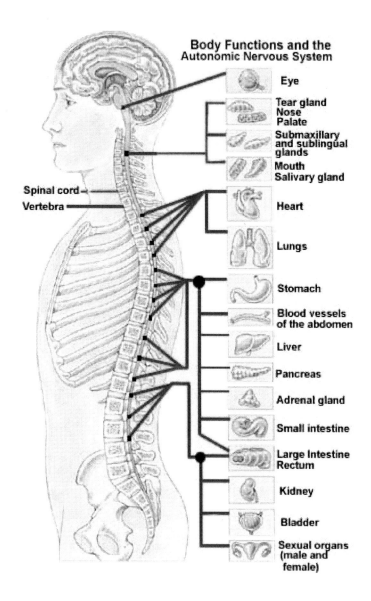

Body Functions and the Autonomic Nervous System

Eye

Tear gland
Nose
Palate

Submaxillary
and sublingual
glands

Mouth
Salivary gland

Spinal cord
Vertebra

Heart

Lungs

Stomach

Blood vessels
of the abdomen

Liver

Pancreas

Adrenal gland

Small intestine

Large Intestine
Rectum

Kidney

Bladder

Sexual organs
(male and
female)

The nervous system is the most important system we have in our bodies. It controls every function that occurs in the body, right down to the cellular level. It controls our voluntary and involuntary systems and system processes. The nervous system controls our heartbeat, breathing and digestive processes, as well as the urinary and reproductive systems. It also controls the way we move, when we move and how fast or slow we move.

It has sensory receptors that detect every possible feeling, sense or stimulation. It detects those that occur internally and externally, like pain, temperature, pressure and chemical imbalances in and on the body.

The brain receives the information, interprets it and decides the correct course of action to take. The nerves that send the information to the brain are called the sensory nerves. Then the brain interprets the stimulation and decides what to do. The interpretation is based on the "writings on our walls". This is the summation of all the experiences, feelings and emotions that we have dealt with since the day we are conceived, both positive and negative. The nerves that send the information to the body are called motor nerves. The motor nerves ONLY travel to 2 places in the body, to the muscles and glands. The brain transmits the information through a complex network of nerves to a specific destination. It knows the exact path to take to reach the correct spot. So…where does it go and how does it know where to go?

Nerves travel to either of two structures; muscles or endocrine glands. When the nerves transmit information to a gland, the gland will secrete the hormones. The muscles contract when the nerves transmit a signal to the muscles,

The brain knows the exact gland, hormone or muscle to contract to respond to the stimulus it received. For example, if we become cold or chilled, receptors detect the cold, tells the brain that we are cold and the brain tells the correct muscles to contract and relax at a fast rate of speed. This is called shivering. The contractions of the muscles create heat and the body warms up.

The endocrine system is the second most important system in the body. It is second because it is controlled by the nervous system.

The endocrine system controls the involuntary systems in the body. It controls our moods, circulation, digestive, urinary and reproductive systems. There are many hormones and chemicals that the endocrine system releases. I will mention some of the important ones here.

It releases a hormone called serotonin, which will help to relax the body. It releases endorphins, the body's natural pain relievers. There are two more hormones that it releases that are very important for understanding the emotional body; epinephrine and norepinephrine.

These are the two chemicals that activate the sympathetic nervous system which is our flight or fight reactions to stress. When we are startled, stressed or scared, epinephrine and norepinephrine is released from our adrenal glands and are secreted into the bloodstream. It travels through our blood and has an effect on many parts of the body. They increase our heart rate, increases our respiration rate, increases the blood pressure and it will slow down or stop our non-essential, non- vital organs, like the digestive system. These are the chemicals that are released when we are stressed out and feeling anxious and overwhelmed. How many people, when asked, would admit that they are stressed on a daily basis? Most people perhaps? Is it any wonder why we have so many digestive issues in the world today?

Another system that the sympathetic nervous system shuts down is the urinary system, our kidneys and bladder and the nerve receptors that detect when we need to relieve ourselves. Remember, they are not totally shutting down but are slowed down because our bodies have another job to do, which is to deal with the stress that we are under. Is it any wonder that there are so many people on kidney dialysis, have some type of kidney disease and are on the transplant list to receive a new kidney? The numbers are staggering when we add these numbers to the numbers of individuals with a host of digestive disorders. COME ON PEOPLE!!! We have to wake up and realize what is REALLY causing our health problems!!! And then we have to TREAT the REAL CAUSE. What we do now is put a bandage and mask the symptoms. We mask the problems by using pain killers, muscle relaxers or even powerful nerve block medications. We "hide" the pain without looking for the cause and attempting to correct it. Is it any wonder to you why people cannot come off their pain medications? It's not a wonder to me. If you don't take away the cause, how can you expect the effect to go away? Another example of masking the cause of a problem can be described this way:

Let's say you come home and find a tremendous amount of water on your kitchen floor. You call a plumber and tell him that your problem is you have water all over your floor. He comes over, inspects it, tells you there is water all over your floor and he can fix it. So he installs a drain in the middle of your kitchen floor. Problem Solved!!! No more water on the floor!!! Yay or Nay?? NAY PEOPLE!!! NAY!! He took care of the effect, not the cause. You see, neither you nor him realized the drain in the sink was clogged and the water was still running! You only told him there was water on the floor. So he took care of that, the effect, not the cause.

WE HAVE TO TAKE CARE OF THE CAUSE!!

So what is the cause? In my opinion, the cause of all physical problems is due to a negative emotion. By the time you are finished this book, you will know the causes, you will know the locations of the body where each negative emotion will appear AND, most importantly, you will know how to take care of the cause and hopefully eliminate the physical problem. This is not a guarantee, but I have seen some amazing things happen to my clients! This is why I want to share it here with you!

If you get stuck and can't get rid of all of your pain, you may need to seek the help of a practitioner of EFT, Emotional Freedom Technique

The previous chapter covered our emotions, beliefs, thoughts and ideas. Thoughts and beliefs are products of our mind, and are a type of stimulus. This is something everyone knows. However, what they don't always realize is that emotions, thoughts and beliefs create a nerve transmission. This nerve transmission will cause a muscle contraction or a hormone to be released. And this is the foundation for this book. This is the information you need to know to allow your body to heal.

The nerve transmission sends a signal; this signal is what I refer to as energy. It is the electricity that runs through the nerves.

To help explain the energy in our body, I'll examine reflexology, the chakras and traditional Chinese medicine.

Chapter Four

Reflexology

In reflexology, it is believed that the energy flows from the top of the head to the bottom of the feet. In the feet, there are corresponding points that reflect the energy at every point in the torso and head. The left foot will correspond to the left side of the body and the right foot, the right side. The sole of the foot will act as a map of the torso.

While palpating the sole of the foot, one could refer to a reflexology foot map and discover which organ may be experiencing some complications. A reflexologist would maintain a steady pressure on the particular spot on the foot until he/she feels the stagnant energy begin to flow again. This will help with the return of the body to a state of well-being.

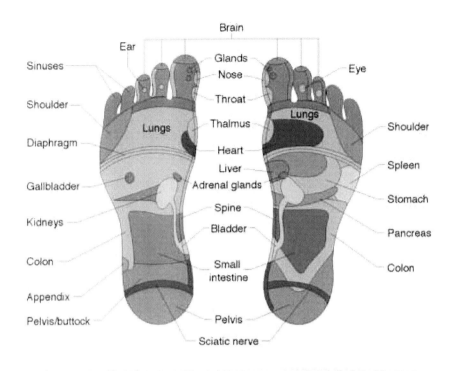

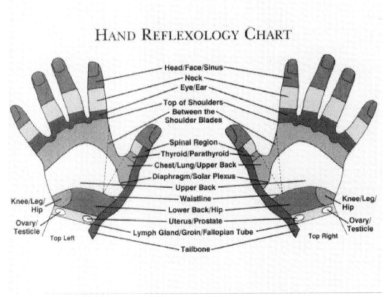

HAND REFLEXOLOGY CHART

Chapter Five

Energy

Everything that is alive pulsates with energy and all of this energy contains information. Your physical body is surrounded by an energy field that extends as far out as your outstretched arms and the full length of your body. It is both an information center and a highly sensitive perceptual system.

We are constantly in communication with everything around us through this system which is a kind of conscious electricity that transmits and receives messages to and from other people's bodies. These messages from and within the energy field are what our intuition can perceive, with practice.

Practitioners of energy medicine believe that the human energy field contains and reflects each individual's energy. It surrounds us and carries with us the emotional energy created by our internal and external experiences - both positive and negative. This emotional force influences the physical tissue within our bodies. In this way your biography - the experiences that make up your life - becomes your biology.

The imagined reality that we project onto our world is related to our "image" of what we concluded the world was like through our childhood experiences; and through the mind of the child we were then. Psychologists say this occurs between the ages of 3 and 8 years old. Since each chakra is related to a specific psychological function, what we project through each chakra will be projected in the general area that each chakra functions and will be very personal to each of us because each person's life experience is unique. By measuring the vibration of the chakras, we can determine one's overall long-term and current life issues.

Experiences that carry emotional energy in our energy systems include:

Past and present relationships (both personal and professional)

Profound or traumatic experiences and memories

Belief patterns and attitudes (including all spiritual and superstitious beliefs)

The emotions from past experiences become encoded in our biological systems and contribute to the formation of our cell tissue, which then generates a quality of energy that reflects these emotions. These energy impressions form an energy language, which carries literal and symbolic information.

If you had an embarrassing experience as a youngster, that experience carried an emotional charge that could have created cellular damage especially if you were to dwell on that memory through adulthood or use it as a touchstone for determining how to deal with criticism, or authority figures, or education - or failure . . .

Positive images and the energy of positive experiences are also held in the energy field. Reflecting on this memory may manifest as a surge of personal power within your body. Your mind is in every cell of your body!

Emotional energy converts into biological matter through a highly complex process. Just as radio stations operate according to specific energy wavelengths, each organ and system in the body is calibrated to absorb and process specific emotional and psychological energy frequencies, i.e., each area of the body transmits energy on a specific, detailed frequency, and when we are healthy - all are "in tune".

An area of the body that is not transmitting at its normal frequency indicates the location of a problem. A change in intensity of the frequency indicates a change in the nature and seriousness of the illness and reveals the stress pattern that has contributed to the development of the illness.

How does one know when a chakra or chakras are not vibrating at normal frequency?

The way to interpret the body's energy is sometimes called "vibrational medicine". It resembles the most ancient medical practices and beliefs, from Chinese disciplines, to indigenous shamanic practices, to virtually every folk or alternative therapy.

There are several ways to discern the state of the chakras. In the universe, all energy flows in a clockwise direction. You can imagine the chakras as a vortex of energy similar to the way a tornado spins. When balanced, the chakra spins in a clockwise direction in a large circle or wheel.

When there is not enough energy in the chakras, the wheel is smaller than normal. If the emotions and thoughts related to that chakra is backwards, reversed or negative, the energy may spin in the opposite direction. If there is too much energy in a chakra, or the thoughts and emotions related to that chakra are overactive, then that chakra will spin in a much larger circle than normal.

One popular method is to use a pendulum. This device helps increase your sensitivities to the energy flow as it acts as an amplifier. The clockwise or counterclockwise motion of each chakra will determine the present state of the chakra.

Clockwise - balanced

Counterclockwise – blockage

Another method is intuitively. Once heightened, intuition will pick up on information that has the strongest impulse - the most intensity. These impulses usually relate directly to the part of the body that is becoming weakened or diseased.

Increasing and continual exhaustion that takes the edge off mental and emotional clarity is any energy symptom that indicates that something is wrong with the body.

If a person is able to sense intuitively that he or she is losing energy because of a stressful situation - and then acts to correct that loss of energy - then the likelihood of that stress developing into a physical crisis is reduced, if not eliminated completely.

The Chakras

The Chakras, however, do have emotions and characteristics associated with them. I will explain the chakra system, as I understand it to work. The Chakras are the energy system recognized by Hindu traditional medicine.

What is a chakra?

Chakra is a Sanskrit word for "wheel". Chakras are often seen by healers and psychic intuitives as spinning wheels of light, vortices, or funnels of energy and are the configuration in the structure of the energy field of the body. In Eastern tradition, the chakras are depicted as lotuses. Their spirals of light indicate the contrasting energies of psyche and spirit: the fiery energies or darker helix contrast with the lighter, spiritual energies and lighter helix, all of which must be brought together in balance. They are more commonly known as the centers of the Endocrine System in Western medical terminology.

There are seven major chakras of the body:

CHAKRA	NO.	ENDOCRINE GLAND	COLOR	FUNCTION
Crown	7	Pineal	Violet-White	Upper Brain, Right Eye
Third Eye	6	Pituitary	Indigo	Lower Brain, Left Eye, Ears, Nose, Nvs System
Throat	5	Thyroid	Blue	Bronchial & Vocal Apparatus, Lungs, GI Tract

Heart	4	Thymus	Green - Pink	Heart, Blood, Vagus Nerve, Circulatory System
Solar Plexus	3	Pancreas	Yellow - Gold	Stomach, Liver, Gall Bladder, Nervous System
Sacral	2	Gonads	Orange	Reproductive System
Root	1	Adrenals	Red	Spinal Column, Kidneys

Each major chakra is located on the front of the body and is paired with its counterpart on the back of the body. Together they are considered to be the front and rear aspect of one chakra. The frontal aspects are related to the person's feelings - the rear ones to his will and the three located on the head - to his mental processes. The following charts describe the location, psychological functions, emotional issues and physical dysfunctions associated with each chakra. Look at the physical dysfunction that you experience, then check to see what chakra(s) are affected and then check to see which emotions you experience. Not all of the options listed will be meant for you, but some of them will describe you exactly.

The body's seven main Chakras

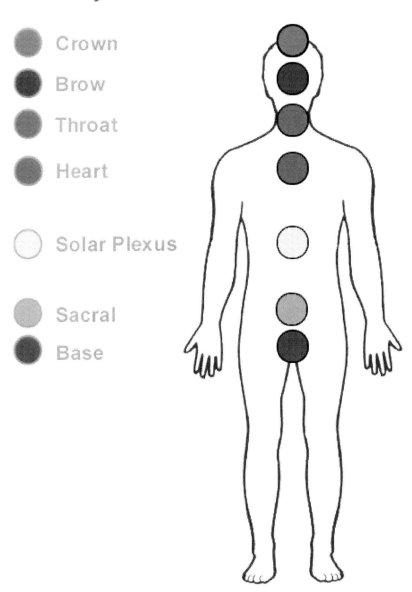

- Crown
- Brow
- Throat
- Heart
- Solar Plexus
- Sacral
- Base

ASSOCIATED PSYCHOLOGICAL FUNCTION

Root chakra - lessons related to the material world

Sacral chakra - lessons related to sexuality, work, and physical desire

Solar Plexus chakra - lessons related to the ego, personality, and self-esteem

Heart chakra - lessons related to love, forgiveness, and compassion

Throat chakra - lessons related to will and self-expression

Third Eye chakra - lessons related to mind, intuition, insight, and wisdom

Crown chakra - lessons related to spirituality

Symptoms of Diseased Chakras

CHAKRAS	ORGANS	MENTAL/EMOTIONAL ISSUES	PHYSICAL DYSFUNCTIONS
Root Chakra	Base of spine, legs, bones, feet, rectum, immune system	Physical family & group safety and security, ability to provide life's necessities, ability to stand up for self, feeling sense of belonging, social & familial law and order	Chronic lower back pain, sciatica, varicose veins, rectal tumors/cancer, depression, immune-related disorders
Sacral Chakra	Sexual organs, large intestine, lower vertebrae, pelvis, appendix, bladder, hip area	Blame and guilt, money and sex, power and control, creativity, ethics and honor in relationships	Chronic lower back pain, sciatica, ob/gyn problems, pelvic/low back pain, sexual potency or lack of, urinary problems
Solar Plexus	Abdomen, stomach, upper intestines, liver, gallbladder, kidney, pancreas, adrenal glands, spleen, middle spine	Trust, fear and intimidation, self-esteem, self-confidence & self-respect, care of self and others, responsibility for making decisions, sensitivity to criticism, personal honor	Arthritis, gastric or duodenal ulcers, colon/intestinal problems, pancreatitis/diabetes, indigestion - chronic or acute, anorexia or bulimia, liver dysfunction, hepatitis adrenal dysfunction

Heart Chakra	Heart and circulatory system, lungs, shoulders and arms, ribs/breasts, diaphragm, thymus gland	Love and hatred, resentment and bitterness, grief and anger, self-centeredness, loneliness & commitment, forgiveness and compassion, hope and trust	Congestive heart failur, heart attack, mitral val prolapse, cardiomegaly asthma/allergy, lung cancer, bronchial pneumonia, upper back shoulder, breast cancer
Throat Chakra	Throat, thyroid, trachea, neck vertebrae, mouth, teeth and gums, esophagus, parathyroid, hypothalamus	Choice & strength of will, personal expression, following your dream, using personal power to create, addiction, judgment & criticism, faith & knowledge, capacity to make decisions	Raspy throat, chronic s throat, mouth ulcers, g difficulties, joint probl scoliosis, laryngitis, swollen glands, thyroi problems
Third Eye Chakra	Brain, nervous system, eyes, ears, nose, pituitary gland	Self-evaluation, truth, intellectual abilities, feelings of adequacy, openness to the ideas of others, ability to learn from experience, emotional intelligence	Brain tumor/hemorrhage/str neurological disturban blindness, deafness, fu spinal difficulties, lear disabilities, seizures
Crown Chakra	Muscular system, skeletal system, skin	Ability to trust life, values, ethics, and courage, humanitarianism, selflessness, ability to see the larger picture, faith and inspiration, spirituality and devotion	Energetic disorders, mystical depression, chronic exhaustion not linked to a physical disorder, extreme sensitivities to light, so and other environment factors

How Thought Affects our Chakra Energy.

The following is the step by step process that occurs when a negative emotion, thought, belief or idea resides in our minds and how it affects our body. I want you to realize that with <u>every thought there is a reaction.</u> This response can either energize you or decrease your life force. For example, when you have a negative thought:

- Negative thoughts cause the electricity of the brain to change.

- Due to the change of the brain electricity, the meridian energy changes.

- The organs connected with the meridian are not properly nourished with vital energy and disease develops.

- The astral energy feedback changes in the chakra due to the bad thought. This thought has less vitality as it is out of the cosmic tune. A block in the chakra occurs.

- Negative thinking drains away the energy of the aura. The colors become dull and the auric protection shield weaker. Negativity from the outside can pour in.

- When negative thoughts are radiated to the environment, all thoughts on that morphogenetic field will be attracted. The negativity becomes stronger and happens more often.

Each chakra center is connected to a level of intelligence that is part of our whole being. The following is a general description of each chakra.

- The Root Chakra is our life force energy. It is also called our Red or Base Center
- The Sacral Chakra is our sensing and feeling energy. It is also called our Orange or Splenic Center
- The Solar Plexus Chakra is our mental energy. It is also called our Yellow or Ego Center
- The Heart Chakra is our emotional energy. It is also called our Green or Cardiac Center
- The Throat Chakra is our communication energy. It is also called our Blue or Laryngeal Center
- The Third Eye Chakra is our intuitive energy. It is also called our Indigo or Brow Center
- The Crown Chakra is our inspiration and spiritual energy. It is also called our Violet or Coronal Center.

Now that you understand the basics of each chakra and the color vibration it correlates to you can begin to work with "tools" that will help energize the chakra center(s) you need to work on. The main tool I ask people to work with is the "right" (positive) thoughts. If you already have doubts or disbelief your end results will be affected in a negative way

. Your thoughts are mainly what drive you on a physical level. It is your mind that tells you what to do, what you should learn and how you should act or re-act. This is why first and foremost you need to put the power of your mind into the thought that you are going to work at increasing your chakra system's vitality. It is simply by acknowledging this that you have taken the first step to empowering your chakras.

As you review the following information about the chakras, try and find yourself and your feelings, emotions, thoughts and beliefs and determine which chakras may be out of tune. Try and be honest with yourself.

1) Root Chakra
2) Sacral Chakra
3) Solar Plexus Chakra
4) Heart Chakra
5) Throat Chakra
6) Third Eye Chakra
7) Crown Chakra

The first chakra is the root chakra. The root chakra is located at the base of the spine, at our tailbone. In general, the root chakra deals with how we relate to the four basic need for survival: Food, Clothing, Shelter and money. It deals with the fears and other emotions we have regarding these items. This refers to an individual who has lost their job, or is afraid they will lose it. Someone who is worried if they have enough money to put food on the table, or pay the mortgage bill, will have problems in the areas governed by the root chakra. . The people who say, "Where will I live" or "What will I eat" or "How will I be able to support myself and/or my family". These are the negative emotions, thoughts and feelings associated with this chakra.

The color of the root chakra is red. The individual may see blotches of red or red shapes when closing their eyes. The lower legs are governed by the root chakra. Those experiencing the above emotions and feelings will have muscle problems and/or pain in the lower legs. If the pain is in the front, like shin splints for example, this person is most likely worried about where the future will be taking them and what will happen to them.

They may also have troubles with their calf muscles, like muscle cramps, or a charley horse. This may indicate a fear of something from the past that perhaps will happen again. It may be that as a child this individual experienced something similar with their parents or someone else in their important in their lives. Perhaps they are remembering the emotions that these individuals went through and saw their suffering. Maybe as a child they took on or felt these same emotions. And now, "It's going to happen to me, I just know it", "I'll end up just like them".

This chakra is all about support. The lower legs support the body as we stand and walk. It also takes us to where we are going. Depending on whether this chakra is opened, closed or reversed depends on how well we feel supported, or whether we think we can support ourselves confidently. It is also about how we stand up for ourselves, "are we on firm ground or will we sink?" When you think of the root chakra, think about it being the foundation for our lives and what items we need for a firm foundation. This Chakra is about "me, myself and I" and how it is going to affect "me" and "what will "I" have to do now.

The second chakra is the Sacral Chakra. The sacral chakra is located at the low back region. From the front, it is at the level of the hips below the navel. In general, the sacral chakra deals with how we relate to other people on an individual basis. It is an expression of our relationship with our partners, siblings, parents, and other relatives. It can also be our association with our jobs, careers or any other organizations to which we belong. It is closely connected to our root chakra and can hold many similarities with it. The upper legs and knees are governed by the sacral chakra.

Those experiencing worries, fears or angers with anyone will experience problems in their upper legs, knees or low back. Having problems in this area will indicate problems, arguments and grudges held towards another person or organization. For example, pain or discomfort in the low back may mean that this person has fear over a relationship with someone.

This chakra controls our reproductive system and our urinary bladder. It reveals our thoughts on sex and sexuality and the emotions that coincide with how we view our sexual experiences. If our libido (sex drive) is over active, then this chakra will be overactive also. We may experience problems with the organs in this area, the ones that are governed by this chakra.

The color of this chakra is orange. When closing the eyes, if shapes or blotches of orange appear, then this chakra is experiencing some type of malfunction in he flow of energy.

The third chakra is the Solar Plexus. The solar plexus is located in the abdomen, above the navel. In general, this chakra deals with how we feel about ourselves and how we relate to society and how we think society sees us. It is our self-esteem, self-confidence and self worth. When we think we are "no good" or we "can't do it, this chakra will be closed or "backwards". And so, these self-deprecating feelings will have a negative effect on the organs, muscles and tissues surrounding this chakra.

Those who doubt themselves and believe they are "no good", or they "won't or can't achieve' a goal or think that they are not important, will have trouble in this region.

They will experience feelings of nervousness; nausea and perhaps vomiting.

Those experiencing anxiety will have stomach problems while those who hold grudges and resentment will have problems in the large intestines. They "hold it in" and "keep it to themselves" so "they" don't feel guilty about being a burden on others.

Those who over analyze every situation, no matter how trivial; will experience problems in the spleen and pancreas. The small intestines job is assimilation of nutrients, the things that are good for us. So, problems in the small intestines would indicate problems of beliefs (absorption of information) and problems of trust, the skeptical.

The organs associated with the solar plexus are the stomach, spleen, small and large intestines, pancreas, gall bladder and liver. The color of this chakra is yellow.

The next chakra is the Heart Chakra. The heart chakra is located in the center of the chest and it is the fourth chakra.. The color of this chakra is green. In general, as you would expect, this chakra deals with love. Love of others and the love of self. It deals with hatred as well as with lost or broken love. When we are separated from the ones we love, we say our "heart is broken". We will experience heart problems because of a lost love, or hatred for someone.

The organs associated with the heart chakra are the heart and lungs. The esophagus and thymus gland are also associated with this chakra. The esophagus will have problems if we "have trouble swallowing" information. The disbelief usually associated with hatred and a lost love. The thymus gland produces and secretes T-cells, the cells that are responsible for fighting disease in our bodies. It is our body's mobile army command center. So, it is of no surprise that the thymus will not function properly if we have "lost our will to fight", or if we are "cowardly' and do not want to stand up for ourselves.

The Throat Chakra is the next in line as we travel towards the head. It is the 5th major chakra of the body. The color of this chakra is blue. Many individuals have problems with the blue chakra. The major characteristic of the throat chakra is communication. It is located near the larynx and voice box.

People who have trouble getting their point across will have stagnant energy in this chakra. Sometimes, we don't like to speak our minds for various reasons. Maybe so as to not offend someone or someone doesn't allow us to speak our minds. For example, a parent may say "Don't talk to me like that" and the child interprets that to mean "you can't say what's on your mind". If your boss is going to yell at you every time you approach them, then we stop approaching them, even when the information you have would be helpful. Perhaps you had an idea that the boss discredited at an earlier time that makes you keep your mouth shut. Being "bottled up" inside creates stagnant energy in the throat chakra.

The organs associated with this chakra are the thyroid gland and the voice box. One of the functions of the thyroid gland is to regulate metabolism. I want you to think of a person you know who "doesn't shut up" and who always "speaks their mind". This person has an active or perhaps even an overactive throat chakra. Since there is a lot of energy in this chakra, it will increase the functions of the organs associated with this chakra. So, that means, these individual will have an increase in metabolism and, since they have been this way for years, they are thin and always hot. They need a window open, even in the dead of winter. They can eat a lot of food and not gain any weight.

The opposite will also happen to individuals that are not as outspoken, the timid ones. These people will not have much energy in this area, and are not prone to say what they are thinking. This will decrease the functioning of the thyroid. Metabolism will be slow and these people tend to be heavier as a result of the decrease. They will be cold even when everyone else is comfortable. Think of your coworkers who constantly turning the heat up, look at their body shapes and then look at their mannerisms. You will begin to see patterns.

I will say one last thing about the throat chakra. Those individuals who seemingly don't have a problem with their weight and who suddenly has difficulties expressing themselves or speaking their minds, will suddenly experience a sore throat, laryngitis or get a throat infection.

The next chakra is the Third Eye Chakra. It is also called the Brow or Forehead Chakra. It is located in the center of the head, between the eyebrows above the bridge of the nose. The color associated with this chakra is Indigo.

The emotional characteristic is intuition, wisdom, understanding and insight. It controls the eyes and the base of the skull. When we "can't see straight" because of anger or other emotion, we will experience problems with the eyes. Maybe we won't "see eye to eye", or "can't see a person truly doing" something.

The last of the seven major chakras is the Crown Chakra. It is located at the top of the head where the soft spot was as a baby. The color of this chakra is violet. This chakra controls the brain and our thoughts and feelings. It is our connection to the spiritual, our higher self.

Many people in this day and age are materialistic. These people have active lower chakras. The individuals that are big thinkers, who have and use their intuition, have active chakras at the higher levels.

If you have been truthful and honest with yourself, you should have learned something about yourself. You would have been able to can see the areas that you can improve in your life. This is the first step in accepting who you are at this moment in time. The next step is to start doing things to manifest more energy in the chakra center(s) that needs more recognition. Don't be concerned if all of your centers need work. Most people do not understand their chakras 100%, but that's why we are here... to learn and to grow!

Chapter Six

Shiatsu and Acupuncture Meridians

For thousands of years the Eastern Asian community has been treating sickness and disease based on Traditional Chinese Medicine. They use a system called the Five Element Theory. This is a very complex system, in which the doctors utilize a wide variety of characteristics to help diagnose an individual's problem. It is my intent, in this chapter, to explain this process in simplified form as to help the reader to understand the philosophy of this theory.

The most important thing to understand concerning traditional Chinese medicine is the Yin/Yang theory. This theory states that the body has opposing yet complimentary forces that keep the body in balance. Each element found in the body has a yin organ and a yang organ.

According to Traditional Chinese Medicine there are 5 elements that are present in the body. They are Fire, Earth, Metal, Water and Wood. Each element has specific characteristics and emotions that it governs and is identified with certain organs and organ systems of the body.

The 5 Element Theory is based on the fact that energy flows through channels, or meridians. The energy flows at specific times in certain places. There are 12 major meridians plus 2 vessels that run up and down the body.

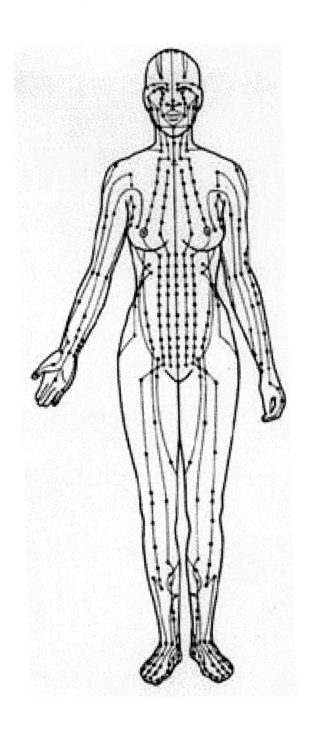

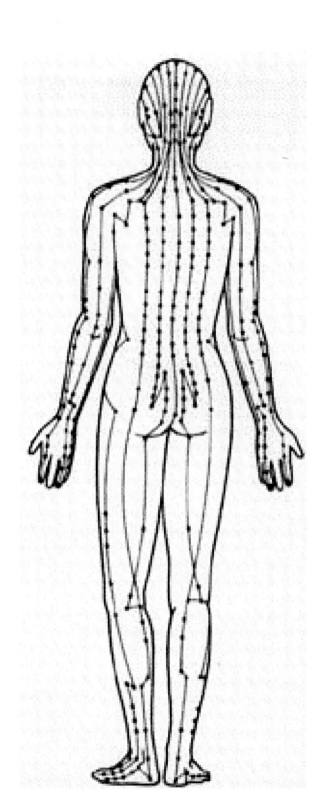

The meridians are named for the organs and organ systems that they happen to pass through. The list of the meridians, according to the way energy flows is as follows: Lung, Large Intestines, Stomach, Spleen/Pancreas, Heart, Small Intestines, Urinary Bladder, Kidney, Pericardium, Triple Warmer, Gall Bladder and Liver.

Energy flows through our body in a cycle. Each cycle lasts 24 hours. Since there are 12 meridians that means the energy spends 2 hours in each meridian.

There are also 2 large vessels in the body: the conception vessel and the governing vessel. The conception vessel runs straight up the center of the body, from the perineum to the crease on the chin. The governing vessel runs from the perineum up the back, around the top of the head and down to just below the nose. The conception vessel is associated usually with our offspring and the governing vessel deals with control.

There are many characteristics that are associated with each element. I have combined the elements and meridians together with the negative emotions, seasons, joints and sensory organs. I have listed them here in the order that energy flows in the body:

The elements associated with the meridians are as follows: Fire – Heart, Small Intestines, Pericardium and Triple Warmer: Earth – Stomach and Spleen/Pancreas: Metal – Lung and Large Intestines: Water – Urinary Bladder and Kidney: Wood – Gall Bladder and Liver.

Fire – excess joy, summer, elbow & tongue
Earth – over-thinking, late summer, hip & mouth
Metal – grief, fall, wrist and nose
Water – fear, winter, knee and ear
Wood – anger, spring, shoulder and eye.

According to Chinese Medicine, energy travels throughout our body constantly and each meridian will reach a peak of energy at a specific time of the day. The following is a list of the meridians in the order that the energy flows throughout the body.

The Metal Element starts us off each day with the Lungs. Energy is in our Lung meridian from 3am to 5 am. Next it travels to the Large Intestine meridian. Energy is in this meridian from 5am to 7am. The Lung is the yin organ and the large intestine the yang.

Both meridians, being a metal element, are associated with the emotions grief, sorrow, sadness and depression. They control or govern the wrist and nose. These meridians are associated with the season of fall.

The Earth organs are the Stomach, which is the yang organ and the Spleen meridian, which is the Yin. It should be noted here that the spleen meridian is also known as the spleen and pancreas meridian, since the energy flows through both organs. It travels through the stomach meridian from 7am to 9am and the spleen meridian from 9am to 11am.

These meridians are associated with the emotions of over-thinking and over-analytical. They control the hip joint and the mouth and the season of late summer, also known as Indian summer.

The Fire element holds 4 separate meridians total, we will review 2 now and 2 later. The first pair are the Heart meridian and the Small Intestine meridian. The heart reaches it peak energy at 11am and it remains there until 1pm. The Small Intestine has its peak from 1pm to 3pm.

The emotion that resides in the heart meridian is the feeling of having a "broken heart". The emotion for the small intestines is the lack of trust or belief.

The Water Element is next, having the Bladder and Kidney associated with that element. The bladder receives its energy first and its peak at 3pm and holds it until 5pm. Then the energy flows to the kidney and remains there from 5pm to 7pm

The emotions that are related to both the bladder and the kidney are fear, worry, apprehension and concern.

The energy then flows back to the Fire element meridians. The Pericardium reaches its peak of energy at 7pm and it lasts until 9pm. Then it goes to the Triple Warmer meridian from 9pm to 11pm. There are other names for the triple warmer meridian. They include triple burner, triple heater and san jaio. Meridian charts will use any of these names, however, it is referring to the same meridian.

The Pericardium meridian also has another name associated with it. It is also called the Circulation/Sex meridian. The pericardium meridian deals with protecting the heart so it doesn't get broken again. Some same we have a hardened heart.

The triple warmer emotion is "not feeling loved" or "unable to feel loved", perhaps because we have closed our heart to the possibility of loving someone else. Or maybe it's when we feel like we have no friends, no one loves us or when we think everyone hates us.

Next, the energy flows to the Wood element, where it finds the Gall Bladder and the Liver respectively. It enters the gall bladder at 11pm and leaves at 1am. At 1am, the energy peaks in the Liver meridian and it stays there until 3am. Then the cycle continues again starting in the Lungs.

The emotions that reside in both the gall bladder and liver are anger, frustration, aggravation, irritation, rage and resentment. Yes, think about someone you know who has had their gall bladder removed. Follow me on this: The gall bladder is a yang organ, according to Chinese medicine. Yang organs refer to the male gender. The emotions are above. Think of the person you know that has had their gall bladder removed and ask them or ask yourself "who is the Male that they were angry, frustrated or aggravated with or who they resented." Now you know why their gall bladder had problems. It is from these emotions.

In a later chapter, I will discuss more in depth how to utilize the information above in order to determine the underlying emotion causing the physical problem, condition or disease. Now, I will give you more information, more possibilities of the emotions of each meridian and what happens if we have an imbalance of energy in the body.

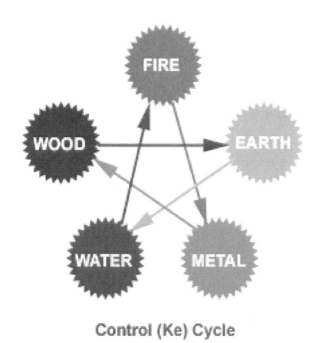

Control (Ke) Cycle

The Five Elements

The Five Elements, or Five Phases, are aspects of Qi (energy). These are Wood, Fire, Earth, Metal, and Water. In the poetic language of the Five Elements, health is a harmonious balance of all the elements. The Qi of the elements waxes and wanes in daily and seasonal cycles. Each one of us is a unique and characteristic blend of the influences of all the elements.

Wood

Meridians: Liver/Gallbladder

People who have strong energy of the Wood element have a clear vision and goals, and know how to bring them into being. They excel at planning and decision making. They can be forceful in disagreements and can strongly argue their opinions. Their piercing, penetrating eyes may attract you, but avoid their wrath.

Wood Imbalance

When the wood Qi is weak, people can be indecisive, without strong direction in life, and stuck. They may be constrained emotionally, unable to express anger. When the Liver Qi is congested or stagnant, people can be arrogant, over controlling, and have angry dispositions. They may have a tendency to be workaholics or have addictive personalities, including the possibility of abusing drugs and alcohol. They may have digestive problems like bloating, gas, alternating constipation and diarrhea.

When Liver Qi is imbalanced, hot and spicy foods may cause too much heat. Sour and bitter flavors are said to benefit the Liver meridian. Excessive frustration and irritation can be especially difficult when the Liver meridian is out of balance. Physical exercise and reading can help restore balance. The fall is a vulnerable time, as well as the winds of March, and extremely hot weather.

Common signs of Liver meridian stress include dry, brittle, thickened nails and pain just below the ribs. Common illnesses include migraines, eye problems, and sinus problems. The Liver meridian circles the genitals, and rashes and discharges are associated with its imbalance, as well as hernias. For women, menstrual problems are common including PMS, painful periods, and heavy bleeding. Uterine fibroids may be related to imbalance of the Liver meridian as well. The Liver and Gallbladder meridian pathways traverse the top and sides of the head, the most common sites for migraines. The Qi of the Wood element flourishes in the spring and the color of this element is green.

Fire

Meridians: Heart, Small Intestines, Pericardium, Triple Warmer

People with strong Fire energy may be quite charismatic. They excel at commanding others to action. They may love talking and socializing.

Fire Imbalance

When the Fire Qi is weak, a person may be lackluster or bland. They may suffer from anxiety, restlessness, and insomnia. They may stutter, talk too much and too rapidly, or laugh nervously. They may be too excitable, easily stimulated to excesses, or they may be emotionally cold and unfeeling.

Common illnesses include palpitations, hypertension, heart problems, and sores on the mouth and tongue. People strongly influenced by the Fire element may be vulnerable in very hot weather, and may be calmed and centered by walking. The bitter flavor favors the Fire Qi. Coffee is a bitter flavor, but its effects may aggravate the Heart Qi. The healthy bitter flavors include dark, green leafy vegetables.

Earth

Meridians: Stomach/Spleen

Someone with well-developed Earth energy is a well-grounded, nurturing, compassionate person, sometimes depicted as the archetypical "earth mother". Earth people like to bring others together and make good mediators or peacemakers and reliable friends. They often enjoy both preparing food and eating. You may be attracted by their generous mouth and full, sensuous lips.

Earth Imbalance

When people have weak Earth Qi, they can be worriers and meddlers. They are prone to pensiveness. They may overwork, especially in studying or other intellectual work. They are vulnerable to digestive problems and diarrhea. They may gain weight easily and lose it with difficulty. Their bodies have a tendency to make excessive mucus, and they may suffer from cloudy thinking, muzzy-headedness, and a lack of clarity.

Those with weak Earth Qi often feel better when they limit cold, raw foods and dairy products. They should eat warming foods and grains to stay well grounded. They may crave sweets. The sweet taste can be satisfied by eating sweet grains, vegetables, and fruits rather than processed sugars.

Common illnesses include: fatigue, diarrhea, gas & bloating, food allergies & sensitivities, eating disorders, heartburn, and canker sores. Excessive mucus may collect in the lungs or in the sinuses. In women, menstrual problems may include either excessively light or heavy periods.

The Qi of the earth element flourishes in Indian Summer, those golden moments of fullness before the waning of the light. The earth color is yellow, like the sun, and the ripened crops, and the root vegetables. Sitting meditation is said to strengthen the earth element.

Metal

Meridians: Lungs/Large Intestines

A person with well-balanced Metal energy is well organized, self-disciplined, and conscientious. They like structure in their life. They are most comfortable in situations when they know the rules and can succeed by following them. Metal Qi bestows a deep inner strength, like ore mined from the mountains.

Metal Imbalance

A person with Metal Qi imbalance may be grief-stricken, steeped in sadness. They may have trouble letting go. When the Metal energy is weak, there can be illnesses of the lungs – asthma, allergies, and frequent colds. The Lung meridian rules the skin, so rashes, eczema, and problems with sweating can manifest. The Large Intestine meridian can be affected by chronic constipation or diarrhea, or other bowel diseases.

The Metal energy peaks in the fall. In autumn, metal people feel they can accomplish anything. The color of Metal is white, and people strongly influenced by the Metal Qi may have pale complexions.

Water

Meridians: Kidneys, Bladder

The Water energy is a strong generative force centered in the lower belly. When the Kidney Qi is strong, a person is fearless, determined, and can endure many hardships in pursuit of their goals. Persevering by will power is characteristic of those with strong Kidney Qi. Longevity is also considered to be associated with healthy Kidney Qi, signified by large, elongated ear lobes, like those of the Buddha.

Water Imbalance

When the Kidney Qi is weak, there can be problems with water metabolism, urination, fertility, or sexuality. This person could be anxious, fearful, and withdrawn, and in more severe cases, phobic.

Kidney Qi declines with aging. There may be diminished hearing or ringing in the ears. In menopause, the Kidney yin declines, which is associated with classic signs of heat and dryness – hot flashes, night sweats, dry skin and mucous membranes? Kidney yang weakness is associated with cold – cold extremities, cold back and belly, declining sexual vigor, urinary frequency or incontinence.

The color of the Kidney is black, like the night, or like black ice. When the Kidney Qi starts to weaken, dark circles or pouches appear under the eyes. The Kidney Qi rules in the winter, a time when living things are contracted with cold. Like a seed deep in the cold ground, Qi is dormant, waiting for the time to sprout.

The following pictures show the 14 major meridians of the body as described by Traditional Chinese Medicine.

The following pictures are reprinted with permission from and are owned by Acupunctureproducts.com

Lung Meridian

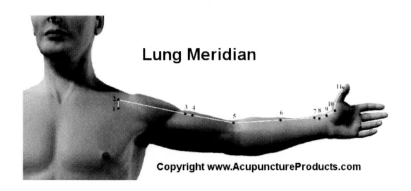

Large Intestine Meridian

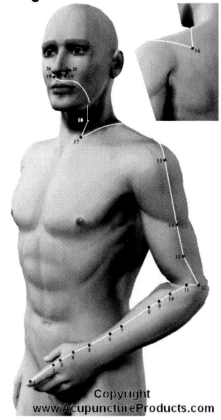

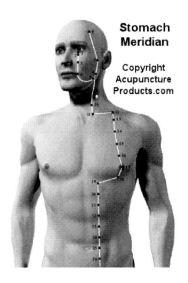

**Stomach
Meridian**

Copyright
Acupuncture
Products.com

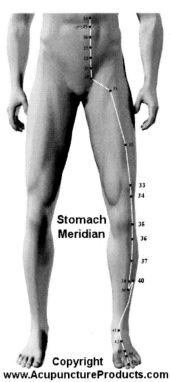

**Stomach
Meridian**

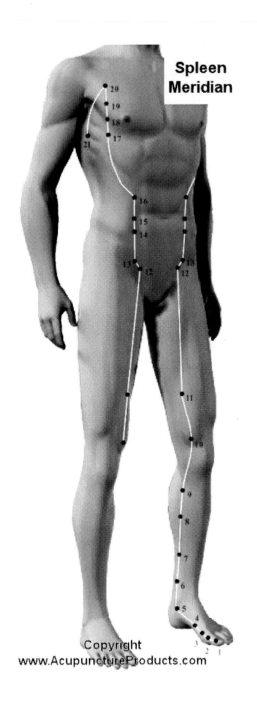

Spleen Meridian

68

Heart Meridian

Small Intestine Meridian

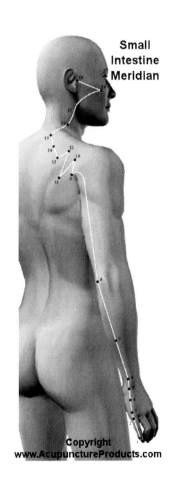

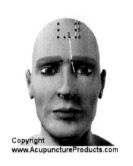

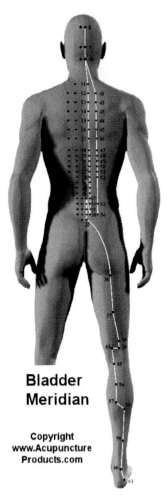

Bladder
Meridian

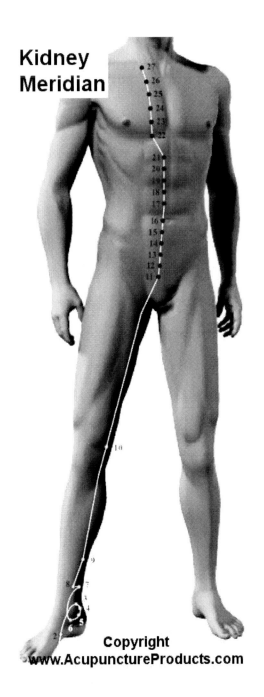

Kidney Meridian

Pericardium Meridian

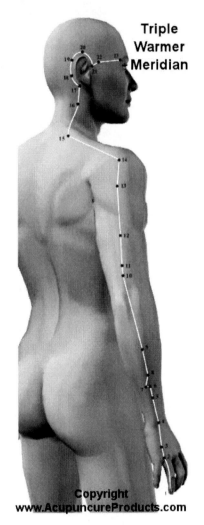

Triple Warmer Meridian

72

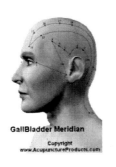

GallBladder Meridian

GallBladder Meridian

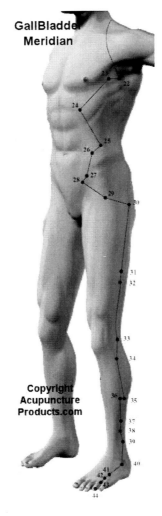

Liver
Meridian

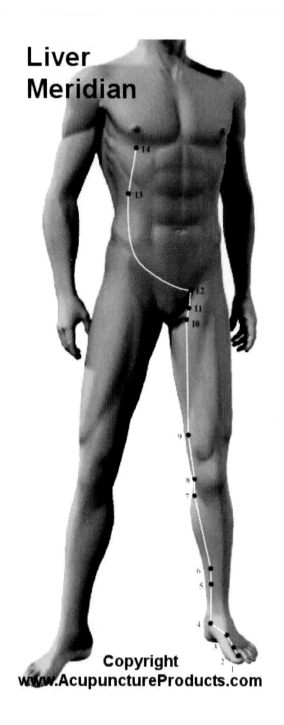

Copyright
www.AcupunctureProducts.com

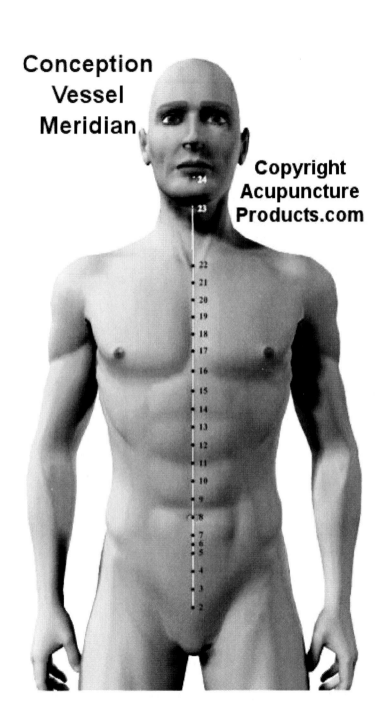

Conception
Vessel
Meridian

75

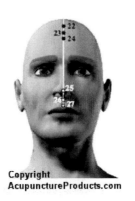

**Governing
Vessel
Meridian**

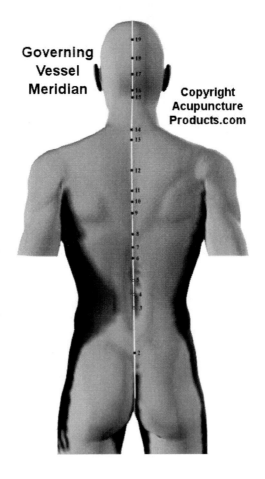

76

Chapter Seven

Literal and Symbolic Meanings

There are many experiences in our lives that have both a literal and symbolic meaning. This hold true to our emotions and how the body "holds onto" these emotions. As you have learned so far, the muscles hold the memory of all of our experiences, good and bad. The good memories help keep our blood flowing regularly and our body works as it should. It is when these emotions have a negative charge, or perhaps I should say when we experience a negative emotion, our muscles store these emotions.

To help you understand the association of the literal and symbolic emotions and how they relate to the body, I will provide some examples. Hopefully this will help you identify the negative emotions in your body and the thought processes that created them.

Literally, our eyes have the sense of sight. We see with our eyes. Most of us move along through life with the ability to "see", we see obstacles in front of us so we can avoid them. Some have lost their sight, or never had it, and so they must cope utilizing other measures to detect obstacles in order to avoid them.

So one negative thought process might be; "I can't see how that could be possible" or "I can't see this or that to be true". Although what you mean to say is "I don't believe it", we use these symbolic sentences to describe our thoughts. The thought of "I can't see the truth to that" or any version of "I can't see...." will manifest a problem with vision and the ability to see.

I had a student come to me and asked for a popular over-the-counter pain medication. I asked what was wrong. He said he had a headache and he couldn't se out of his right eye. I asked when it started and he replied that it had begun that morning. As a massage therapist, I know that headaches and even migraines are caused by tight muscles in your neck pressing against nerves, which cause pain to radiate into the head. And so I wanted to show him that we could get rid of his headache a different way.

I told him that emotions cause physical pain, symptoms and medical conditions and that I believed what he was experiencing was caused by a negative emotion. I began using the "Tap It Out" technique as I told him what the emotions were that he was experiencing. During the "Tap It Out" technique, you tap on the 14 meridians in the body while thinking, speaking and feeling the emotions that are causing the symptoms or conditions. We will discuss this technique later in the book.

I informed him that he had a conversation with a male recently, perhaps the day before, that he "couldn't see" the person telling the truth, that he didn't believe what the man was saying. It needed to be a male since it was his left eye that was affected. I asked him if he had this conversation and to elaborate. He said that his estranged father contacted him and wanted to be a part of his life again. Every time that his father appears in his life he asks for money. He told his father these feelings and he tried to assure him that this was not the case this time, that he truly wanted to be a part of his life and see his grandchildren. Of course, this student couldn't "see" that the father was sincere.

This thought process about his father is very strong because of the past experiences of emotional pain he had endured over the years. Along with not being able to see, the eyes hold fear, anger and resentment for what a person "sees" for the future. Note how this would apply in this case. He "foresees" the father asking for money, not paying it back and continuing a cycle that has plagued him for most of his life.

The entire time he is relating this story to me I am "tapping it out". While he is describing in detail the story of his father and the feelings he has towards him, the negative transmission that is running in his meridians and chakras are being rebalanced, which helps the body return to a normal state. Please note that we are not distracting him from his emotions, we are not erasing the memory of any of the experiences in his life. We are getting rid of the negative reaction the body experiences due to the change in the electrical transmission of the thoughts and feelings. We are tapping out the reaction to the memory, thoughts and feelings.

When he finished his story, which was about 15 minutes later, he told me his headache went away and his eyesight returned to normal.

Another popular negative saying is "he or she is a pain in the neck" (or insert other parts of the anatomy here! Guess where you will have pain show up; in the neck! The reason is because you called it into being. This is the law of attraction in action!

The digestive system is a perfect example of how literal and symbolic thoughts and ideas affect the body. When we eat, our mouth and teeth chew up our food until it is ready to swallow. As we swallow, the food bolus enters the stomach where it meets with gastric enzymes that are used to break down the food. As it leaves the stomach, it enters the small intestine. This is where we do the most of our digestion and where absorption of the nutrients occurs. After we extract everything that we need from the remnants of the food, the waste continues through the track into the large intestines. The waste is anything that is not digestible and not good for the body, it is toxic. We must rid our bodies of this horrible substance.

Now let's revisit this pathway to discover the symbolic meanings and the negative thoughts and emotions that are related to the digestive system. First, we take something in. That something is information we are given during a conversation. We take that information and process it. First, as we are listening, we chew it up. Did you ever say "well that's a little hard to swallow"? You literally didn't swallow or even chew up anything tangible. Yet we say it with the intent to say we are not sure if we want to believe it. It is so unbelievable that we don't even want to swallow it!

And if you do "swallow it", it "may not sit well with you". Hmmm. You might not be able to "stomach it". Sounds like you are about to heave, right? Right! You will if this is the thought that is going through your head!

Once we do stomach it, the small intestines absorb it, or should I say, we are deciding if we want to make it a part of us, if we want to accept it in its entirety, or believe or trust the person. Do we take this as the truth or do we "dump it" because it's a bunch of "crap"? This is why the small intestines hold trust and belief, or should I say the lack thereof. Do we "hold on to" negative emotions, thoughts, beliefs or ideas? These are a waste (of time and energy) and are as toxic as the waste in our large intestines. If we do "hold it in", then we become constipated. We must flush our body and systems of the waste that builds up.

If I committed to writing down all of the possible scenarios of the body parts and their corresponding literal and symbolic meanings and the all the possible emotions that they could possibly represent, it would produce incalculable volumes the likes of which would create an overwhelming feeling for the reader. It is my hope that these examples will assist the reader in interpreting for themselves the symbolic meaning of every body part including the blood, tendons, organs, veins and arteries.

The ears are easy. Anger and the willingness to hear or listen to someone are the emotions that reside in the ears. Do you know someone who did have their hearing but they experienced a progressive loss of hearing in one of their ears? If it had been the left ear, then it was a female who they no longer wished to listen to what she had to say. If it was their right ear, a male was involved. Ask the person to give you the date, as close as they can come up with, they lost their hearing. Then ask them what happened 1 or 2 months prior to that date in which they can remember they didn't want to listen to someone or hear what they had to say. You will see that they will have an answer for you.

The eyes are what we are afraid to look at, refuse to look at or see OR are angry at how we see or perceive the future will be.

Our legs "support" us, carry us forward in life, it is about "taking the next step" in our lives.   It is also about "how are we supposed to continue through life either with or without someone very important in our life, someone who we "lean on" and perceive that we cannot live without.

The ribs and chest not only "protect our heart" but it is our "shield" that protects us from getting hurt emotionally by someone. They protect us because we had been hurt by someone in the past, we had our "heartbroken". Some people protect themselves by keeping this shield in place so we don't "let anyone into our heart" so they can't hurt us or break our hearts again.

Now that you know how the body stores emotions, let's see the relationships with other parts of the body and the emotions, thoughts, beliefs, feelings or ideas that are stored in them.

Chapter Eight

Taking on someone else's stuff

So you ask "What if I am not experiencing that emotion or anything like it? What if it doesn't sound like that is what's going on? What if I didn't experience what this book says I did?

Just because it doesn't sound right doesn't mean you calculated anything the wrong way. You are not wrong. Remember this, you are only interpreting what the body says it is experiencing. The body is never wrong. The body is experiencing just as this book describes. Here is the main reason why our bodies would be holding an emotion that doesn't make sense:

IT IS NOT OUR EMOTION! Wow! What did he say? It's not our emotion? Then why is it in MY BODY!? It is because we are empathic and sympathetic to other people's experiences and situations. We may "feel bad" for them or wish to "take these problems away" from someone. Maybe we really "feel" for them.

How did this all start? Why do we take on other people's emotions? The simple answer is, we care. It is a wonderful way to treat someone, with care. With care comes love, so we love these people, even if they are strangers. Every year millions of dollars is donated to charities and causes. Why? It is because we care. So here is what happens. We see someone in a bad condition, we imagine ourselves in that same position, and voila!, we take on another person's emotions. We feel what they feel. We put ourselves in their shoes, how would we feel it that happened to us? We say we can't imagine how we would react or what we would feel, but it's not true. By this time we have already felt the feeling and experienced the emotions that this other person is experiencing. We soaked it up! WE ARE TAKING ON THEIR PROBLEMS, emotional, yes, but also physical.

Your body doesn't know the difference between someone else's emotions and yours. It detects the emotions and feelings and then holds onto it. As stated in chapter three, the brain detects these emotions and feelings, which is a nerve stimulus, and creates a nerve impulse, which travels down a nerve to either of 2 places, a gland or a muscle. The gland would release a hormone or chemical in the body which will have some type of affect. Or it will send a signal to a muscle to tell it to contract, which then could cause a nerve to be trapped which causes pain. Muscles have memory, but what does it remember? Everything that we have experienced since the day we were conceived!

So when do we start taking on people's energy? We start taking on energy right from the womb, as a fetus. We share everything with our mother, or she with us. She shares her blood, nutrients, toxins, waste and positive and negative energies.

As a child, did your mother ever say to you "put yourself in their shoes" or "how did you think that made them feel" or "walk a mile in their shoes before you judge them". Maybe you listened to her. Maybe she said "get upstairs and think about what you have done". Maybe you did think about it. Maybe it made you sad, or upset. Maybe you COULD feel someone else's loneliness or heartache.

The first time you "put yourself in their shoes is when you learned to take other's energies for your own. It is ok to feel bad for someone, but we have to be aware not to take on other's emotions. Yes, it is easier said than done. You need to "block" the emotion and consciously stop yourself from taking it all on.

So, to answer the question that started this entire chapter, What if it doesn't sound like my stuff? Then it is not your stuff! See how simple that answer is? So the TRUE question is "Whose is it!?"

Start thinking about the emotions just as you had found them and described them. Who does it sound like? Who was talking to you shortly before you started to experience these symptoms that shared with you the emotions that you came up with? You will think of it. You will think of it because that is what happened.

In one way, it is not good to take on another person's energy. We may not always be aware that we are doing that. We think we are just "feeling sorry" for them. When we take on another's energy, we can and will experience their physical conditions as well. For example, as a massage therapist, I am constantly in contact with numerous people who come to relieve their stress, take a load off or simply to just relax and unwind after a long, frustrating day. People get massaged to reduce their stress level. So, if that goal is achieved, them where does their stress go, into thin air? Another dimension? It has to go somewhere. If I am not careful, it will come into me. I could take on your tight shoulders, low back pain or foot pain. If you receive a massage because you are having a bad headache and the therapist is able to relieve it, your therapist may get that headache later in the day or that night.

In another way, it IS good that these are someone else's emotions. It is good because we are not "attached" to those emotions. This will make it easier to remove them from our bodies. When the emotions are our own, they become embedded into our bodies, cells and our dna much deeper than someone else's emotions. So the tapping procedure towards the end of this book will help get rid of it quicker.

All of these symptoms have developed because of the stress and worries of today's society. These stressors cause the physical conditions we have today.   In this day and age we have many medical conditions, diseases and things we may call plagues. These "plagues" differ from plagues that were around hundreds of years ago. This is because we have new things to worry about, different thoughts, emotions, beliefs, etc. If people don't realize these emotions are causing all these problems, if they don't realize that there is a simple way to relieve themselves of all of these conditions, then in the future there will be diseases and plagues in which we have never seen before.

We need to be careful with today's society and taking on other people's emotions. For example, we have Facebook. There is SO much drama on Facebook. People want to "dump" all of their problems into cyberspace and have other's feel badly for them. Misery loves company, they say. When you are scrolling through your newsfeed, do you find yourself enraged, sad, lonely, depressed, angered, frustrated or anything else? Do you find feeling sympathy for the person? Be careful not to take their problems on for yourself!

Movie and television producers understand this entire process of making you "feel" the emotions of the people in their stories. They try and tug on your heartstrings in movies that make us sad and cry along with the actors, like in Old Yeller. Or they get you all fired up in revenge in some action movies. There is always a movie that we love that has a "good guy" getting back at the "bad guy". It makes us feel like we helped them get the bad guy; it gets us to feel those emotions of vengeance and justice.

It is similar with our pets. Did you ever notice that your pet is fully aware of when we are not feeling well? What happens? It comes up close to you, sits on your lap or next to you. Your pet senses you are sick and would like to help you feel better. I believe that pets were put here to make us happy, to give us something to care about, allow us to feel and learn about unconditional love. I believe they are also here to help take some of our problems away from us. How do I come to this theory? I have noticed that our pets are having the same medical conditions that their owners have arthritis, diabetes, osteoporosis, etc.

Doesn't it seem that we may be making everyone around us sick? And that brings us to a question you may have regarding babies.

The question may be "If physical problems develop because of an emotion, then why are babies born with physical problems?"

I am going to tell you the answer to this question but this will not be easily heard by parents of babies born with medical conditions.

In the beginning of this chapter I said "Muscles have memory, but what does it remember? Everything that we have experienced since the day we were conceived!"

We remember EVERYTHING that we have experienced since the day we were CONCEIVED! That means that a baby in the womb of its mother will experience everything that the mother experiences during her pregnancy, starting with conception.

I already taught you how we take on another person's stress. These people are strangers and we are able to take on their problems. When our family members experience joy, sadness, anger, frustration, happiness or grief, we can take on their emotions and problems much easier. Why? Because we love them. We have a closer relationship to our siblings, parents, grandparents and off springs. When they hurt, we hurt. We even say things like "this is going to hurt me more than it will hurt you".

But what about babies? There is no closer connection from one individual to another than the baby and its mother. This is the strongest relationship possible. We know and understand that the baby receives everything in utero that it needs to survive, blood supply, oxygen and nutrients. It also experiences the same emotions as the mother.

Let's get back to the original question, "Why are babies born with diseases and medical conditions?" The answer is because the mother experienced some type of emotional trauma during the pregnancy that caused the disease. Think about that for a minute. Put this book down and really think about what I just said.

I told you this would be hard for someone to hear. No one wants to hear or even think about the fact that they were the cause of someone's disease. But that's not what I said. I said that the baby took on the emotions of the mother, and these emotions cause the physical condition. You see, the baby hasn't learned how to deal with stress, it doesn't understand what is going on. But the energy signals that run through the body when we are experiencing some type of emotional trauma cause the energy in the cells to change and act differently. The cells begin to change their shape, their makeup and the way they develop. And this is what causes the conditions that we see in the world today.

We need to learn exactly what this book is trying to teach us. And that is; we have the ability to change the energy frequency in our cells. And changing these frequencies will allow the cell to perform the way they are supposed to perform.

Chapter Nine

The Law of Attraction

I know this is a lot of information that I am giving you. The fact is, your body is a complex system. Remember: everything is energy, matter doesn't exist. When placed under a microscope, everything is energy, energy with a particular frequency. Since it is complex I need to give you enough information for you to completely understand how I have come to know the way our bodies work. It is very important for you so you can figure out the cause of your own conditions and that of your loved ones.

The title of this chapter sums up our discussion here. The Law of Attraction. The law of attraction says that "Like attracts like". Have you ever heard of the following sayings: "birds of a feather flock together", "misery loves company", "laugh and the world laughs with you"? These sayings refer to how we feel and with whom we want to hang around. It means that what we want, we attract, or, better yet, what we attract is due to the thoughts, feelings and beliefs that we have. Everything that our life is about, everyone that is a part of our lives, we have attracted to us through our thoughts. Whether or not you like your job, you attracted it to yourself.

Happiness has its own frequency, as does sadness. When we are happy, we attract those experiences that make us happy. When we are sad, we attract things that make us sadder. Everything on that same morphogenetic field will be attracted. It is in this way that we are creating our future. If you are happy with your job, you will be successful. If you don't like your job, quit. Find something you like to do, something that will make you happy and do it. If you remain in that dead end, horrible job, you will attract sadness, resentment and regret.

I believe that we attract experiences into our lives. I also believe that mosquitos, for example, "attack" us because it is attracted to the energy that is being emitted from our bodies when we are feeling these emotions. Here is how I perceive it:

The mosquito bites us and extracts blood from our veins. But why does it bite us in that particular spot? Why does it not bite us in another part of our body? Why does it seem that they only bite certain people? I'm sure you know certain people that get "eaten alive" by mosquitos. When you are with friends and some are getting bit and some are not getting any bites, there MUST be a reason! The reason is because the mosquitos are being attracted to the ones who have negative energy emitting from their bodies. These individuals have a lot of emotions that they are dealing with and most likely, trying to hide from others. These energies run through our meridians and chakras and then are emitted from our bodies into the atmosphere.

The cause of the increased amount of energy in that particular meridian is the negative emotions associated with that particular meridian are prevalent and increased. Here is an example. People who get bit by a mosquito on the outside ankle and the lower leg area are experiencing anger, resentment, aggravation or frustration at either themselves or someone else for not having enough money to support them or they are angry about having to "move into the future" without that person and their monetary support or "take the next step".

I had a massage therapy student come to class one day, about 2 weeks before graduation, with a sore ankle. He had twisted his right ankle on the curb the day before. Was this a fluke or did he attract this injury? Was it an accident, coincidence or did it happen for a reason? Well, I'll tell you this; there is no such thing as a coincidence. Everything happens for a reason.

So, follow me on this. The ankle holds fear, the legs move us forward in life, and we take the next step. The right side of the body refers to a male. When we put just this together we get "he is afraid to take the next step". Maybe in his mind he is thinking "how am I going to be able to do this"? Do we even know what "this" is? Yes we do. Remember, he is graduating in 2 weeks and he will be a massage therapist. He currently has a different job, he came to school to learn a new profession, and now he is graduating. How is he going to take the next step by transitioning into this new career while making enough money to support his lifestyle?

Now do you see why he attracted his twisted ankle? His thoughts are twisted. He is afraid he won't be able to pull this thing off. He is worried about "falling flat on his face". Do you think there was a chance that when he twisted his ankle he could have "fallen on his face'? This was his thought! He thought he would fail at switching careers and have to remain in a job that he didn't like. As you read this book and learn where the emotions are located in the body and how the body speaks to us, you will come to understand why we get hurt, get mosquito bites, get acne and have diseases and sicknesses. The wonderful thing is, now that we know the negative emotion that caused him to twist his ankle, we have to "tap it out" so he doesn't get hurt again and to allow this twisted ankle to heal much faster!

Chapter Ten

Putting It All Together

The following pages are very important in determining the emotional cause of a person's physical complaints. First, take the signs and/or symptoms and look at the following pages. Be sure to check out which meridians and which chakras are involved. Then find everything that is associated with the meridians, the location on the body and get the information from each of the pages and write it all down.

I will list the information about the next 7 pages so you know what each is representing.

A simple way for me to explain how I come up with the story of the emotions, the story of your life is that I take the intersection of the meridians and the chakras and combine that with the emotions associate with each as well as the meanings of the anatomical body and the metaphysics of the body.

In an attempt to show you the meridians as it is on the body, and for you to be able to identify the locations of each, I had to break the meridians down into 3 separate charts.

Page 99 shows the horizontal locations of the chakras. Each chakra controls all the nerves, blood vessels and organs in each section as described on this page.

Page 100 shows just the gall bladder and the liver meridians.

Page 101 shows just the spleen, small intestine and triple warmer meridians.

Page 102 shows all the rest of the meridians: the lung, large intestine, stomach, heart, bladder, and kidney and pericardium meridians.

I want you to find the location on the body where your pimple, mosquito bite, acne, rash, injury, cut or bruise or whatever and determine which meridian it lies on. As you can tell, the kidney, spleen and liver meridians are very close and criss cross each other in the legs. To figure out exactly which it is, you may need to refer to the pictures of the meridians which are on pages 66 to 76.

Page 103 shows the metaphysics of the body. Each location of the body has a corresponding emotion; feeling or meaning that is particular to it.

Page 104 shows the emotional meanings of the chakras and the meridians.

Page 105 shows the emotional meaning of each meridian.

Pages 106 and 107 show the energetic meanings of the anatomical body. This page is a further breakdown of the body and what each subsection means.

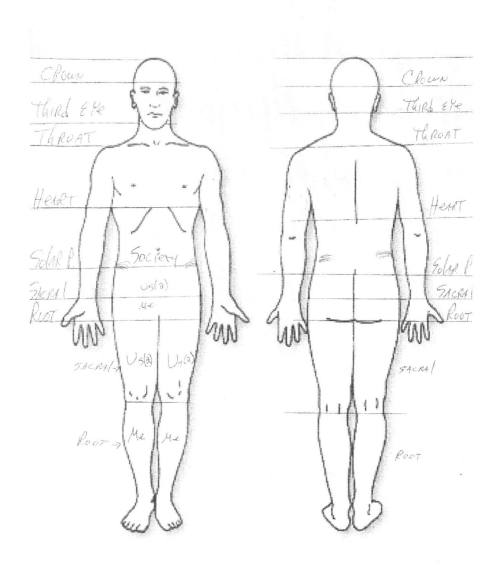

GB , LV

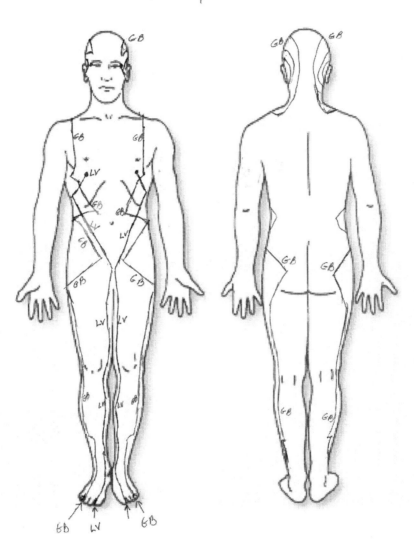

SP, SI, TW

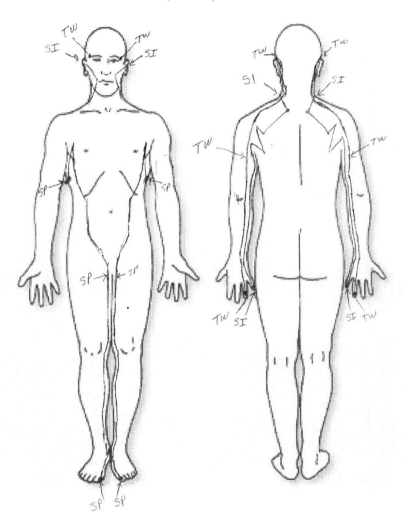

LU, LI, ST, HT, BL, KI, PC

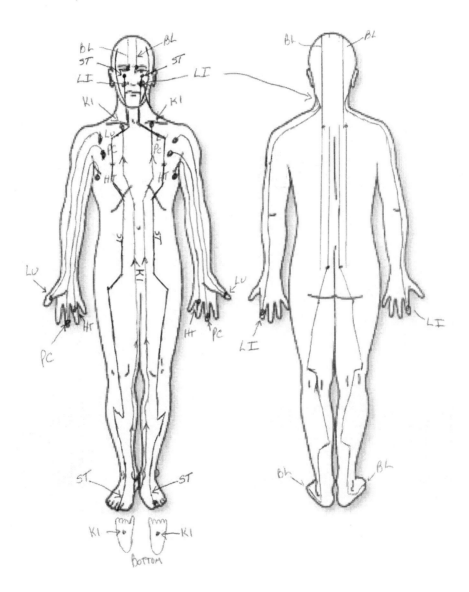

Metaphysics and the Body

The left side of the body
Feminine, emotional

The right side of the body
Masculine, assertive

The Face
What we show to the world
Individuality, persona, mask

Eyes
What we're willing to see or not see

Ears
What we're willing to hear or not
hear

Mouth
Gateway for taking in as well as
expression of mind, having a voice

Neck
Gateway between the head & heart
Balance, flexibility

Shoulders
That which carries and supports
Willingness to know or not know
Responsibility, weight on shoulders

Arms
Our capacity to embrace life

Elbows
Changing directions in life,
flexibility

Hands
The ability to grasp and handle life
Expression of emotion
Fists… anger and resentment

Upper back
Protection – stabbed in the back
Safety and support
Fear of giving or receiving love
Trust issues, feeling betrayed

Mid back
Fear of being taken advantage of,
guilt

Low back
Fear of scarcity
Fear of not being able to support
one's family or lifestyle

The chest
Safety in giving and receiving love
Protecting the heart so no one can
break our heart again

The midriff or belly
How we deal with emotions

Feet and lower legs
Our ability to stand up for ourselves
Ability to move forward in life
Taking the next step
Standing up for what we believe in

Breasts
Nurturing ourselves or others
Giving too much of ourselves
Giving love but not feeling loved

Thighs & Knees
Flexibility, pride, ego
Dealing with authority
Fear of moving forward in a
relationship

Emotional Meanings of the Chakras

Root – Survival, money, food, clothing, shelter, work, job. It's about how it affects "me".

Sacral – Sexuality, partnerships, relationships. It's about how it affects "you and me".

Solar Plexus – Self-Esteem, self-confidence, self-worth. How we think society views us. It's about pleasing others instead of ourselves.

Heart – Love, forgiveness, passion. It's the emotional part of us.

Throat – Communication, creativity, self-expression. Usually we hold back telling others our opinions and feelings. We "hold it in".

Third Eye – Intuition, understanding, wisdom, inner knowledge. It's the knowing without being taught, the understanding without being said.

Crown – Spirituality, our connection to our higher self, our connection to one greater than us

Emotional meanings of the meridians

Lung – grief, sorrow, sadness or depression, "holding in the sadness"

Large Intestine – grief, sorrow, sadness, depression, "holding it in"

Stomach – overthinking, over-analytical, overly detailed, people with OCD, anxiety

Spleen/Pancreas – overthinking, over-analytical, overly detailed, people with OCD, anxiety

Heart – emotional part….broken-hearted, empty heart

Small Intestine – problems with "believing someone", trust issues

Bladder – fear

Kidney – fear

Pericardium – "protecting" the heart, not letting anyone in, closed heart

Triple Warmer – not feeling loved

Gall Bladder – Anger, frustrated, aggravated, irritated, mad, rage

Liver – Anger, frustrated, aggravated, irritated, mad, rage

Governing Vessel (du) – about "control", fear of losing it, always has to have control, upset about not having it at that moment

Conception Vessel (ren) – pertains to sexual issues and attitudes, relationship issues and problem with children

Energetic Meanings of the Anatomical Body

The Front of the Body = the future

The Back of the Body = the past

Face = how we "face" the world, what we show, how we see the future

Front and Side Neck = worry, usually about money

Center of Shoulders = feeling over-whelmed or being dumped on, the "weight of the world on my shoulders", much responsibility

Chest = if it's hard, it's a "shield" to protect & close heart. If it's soft then they are "open" and "vulnerable"

Abdomen = overthinking of or anxiety for the future or self-confidence issues

The side of the ribcage = overthinking about sadness & broken heart, not feeling loved

The Front of the Upper Arm = "carrying" people or emotions

The Front of the Forearm = holding onto something, can't let go, wanting to pull someone or something back, broken heart and sadness, many times about someone dying

The Side of the Upper Arm = someone was taken away from me

The Inside of the Upper Arm = protecting the heart so no one can come in

The Front of the Thigh = future of a relationship (not necessarily romantic) & how it affects "us"

The Front of the Lower Leg and Foot = taking the next step, moving on, standing up for oneself, "having a leg to stand on" and how it affects "me"

Upper Back = lack of trust, feeling of being stabbed in the back

Mid Back = feeling guilty about something

Low Back = fear of not having financial support for "us" (family)

The Back of the Upper Arm = not feeling loved

The Back of the Lower Arm = having to "let go", being forced to let go

Glutes = long-lasting anger, from the past, may be always had anger at "everyone", may be one person or many, deep rooted, most likely from someone they trusted

The Back of the Thigh = fear of repeating something negative from a past relationship "here we go again!"

The Back of the Lower Leg = fear of repeating a past financial instability, "this happened before and it looks like it might happen again"

The Side of the Upper Leg = anger about the relationship

The Inside of the Upper Leg = overthinking about the relationship

The Outside of the Lower Leg = anger about money, support or stability or lack of any of these

The Inside of the Lower Leg = overthinking about money, support or stability or lack of any of these

I know, that's a lot of information and it might seem overwhelming. Let's look at this slowly so you get an idea as to how to use this book as a reference guide to your own emotions.

As stated on page 14, a pimple that shows up somewhere on the body is showing you that there is a buildup of energy until it finally explodes. The energy builds because something is **holding it in**.

Imagine this pimple shows up on the face of a man, on the left side on his cheekbone. Start on page 100 and note that the left side of the body refers to a **female**. Notice the cheekbone is directly below the eye. Also on page 100 it states that the eyes are what we are willing to **see**. Go to page 64 and find the picture of the stomach meridian and that it starts on the cheekbone, in the exact spot of the pimple.

Then go to page 102 and see that the stomach meridian refers to **overthinking, over-analytical, overly detailed, people with OCD**. Since the stomach is the seat of anxiety, we will put the feeling of anxiety here as well.

Then go to page 103 where it talks about the front of the body refers to the **future** and the face is **how or what we show to the world**.

Now go to page 96 and note that the cheekbone is under the control of the third eye chakra, about our inner knowledge of things of the future.

Yes, a simple pimple is holding all of this information. So now we make a sentence or scenario as to what this man's thoughts are that are causing this pimple to appear.

He is overthinking about how he sees the future with a particular woman. Or he is having a lot of anxiety for what he sees as his future with this woman. Maybe he is thinking about how his future would look if he keeps this person in his life for a while. He may be thinking about what others will think (what we show the world) with him being with this woman.

So you see, just because this guy is obsessed with thinking about this situation, the pimple forms on his face. And, this is the same explanation for anyone with a pimple, scratch, rash, bruise, cut or any type of blemish or problem in the same exact spot on the cheekbone.

We'll do another example.

Let's take a woman this time that is having sciatica type pain on her right side. It starts in her butt and travels down the back of her thigh.

First we go to page 97 and we see that the area is controlled by the gall bladder meridian. The emotion is on page 102 and we see anger, frustrated, aggravated, irritated, and mad and rage. It is on her right side, page 100, which is male related. It is on the back of the body which refers to the past as stated on page 103.

Page 104 shows that the gluteal region refers to a "long lasting anger, deep rooted". A slang word for the glutes is ass. Sometimes we say that another person is a "pain in the ass". And now, this woman has a pain in her ass. Yes, this is where her problem originated.

This pain also includes the back of the thigh, which we find on page 104 the following; fear of repeating something negative from a past relationship "here we go again!"

Here is what is happening in her life: Whoever this guy is that is a 'pain in her ass' is someone close to her, brother, father, son, husband, boyfriend or very good friend. Whenever something shows up near the hips, I say that it refers to someone to whom we are "attached at the hip".

Not only this but "here we go again!" This same person has done this to her on a few occasions and now is doing it again. Or it is a different person but is reminding her and her body of the previous times this has happened to her.

For example, if it refers to a boyfriend then perhaps whenever she is in a relationship her boyfriends are always doing the same thing, like flirting, cheating on her, mistreating her, degrading her or maybe they all play jokes on her. Whatever it is, she always finds these types of men. They all become a pain in her ass.

It could refer to her brother. Maybe while growing up he always did something or said something to her, like demeaning her and now she has just seen him recently and he did it again. Her body is remembering all the times in her life that he has done this to her.

Let's say it is her husband. The majority of times, in my experience, her husband is doing the same thing, unbeknownst to him, that her father has done either to her or her mother. Here we go again! Maybe she just realized she 'married her father!'

For me to try and list all possible scenarios on all possible situations and diseases would cause this book to swell to a size of unmanageable conditions. However, I will continue with future books going over more scenarios so you can see how this body of ours is so amazing!

Another book that I will write will show you how to rid yourself of these physical problems by getting rid of the emotions!!

Now try reading your own body to practice what you have learned here in this book. Make a list of all the emotions and feelings in which you become aware about yourself.

In my next book I will show you how to help yourself, using various techniques, to help you heal.

Until then, if you visit a Reiki practitioner or an acupuncturist, meditate, focus and think of one or two of the emotions or feelings from which you wish to heal while you are in your session and youcan start your healing process!

So now you have the pertinent information necessary for you to help yourself heal. The emotions and feelings that you have found regarding yourself have and are, in my opinion, causing your physical problems. You can go to my website, www.EdPortleyJr.com/EFT and download the tapping handout. Follow the instructions and feel better!

Negative emotions cause all bodily ailments, conditions and diseases

I am in touch with my inner guide
I trust my intuition to guide + protect me
I know all is well in my world
I am connected to my Divinity
amethyst, azurite, blue sapphire

Emotional Freedom Technique (EFT
    www.Emofree.com.

Neuro-Emotional Technique-

When you hold something in - you stop energy flow.
Empaths - people that suck up other peoples
        negative energies

Emotions\Beliefs control the body
Nerves travel to: muscles + endocrine system.
With every thought there is a reaction.
Your thoughts are what drives you on a physical level
    So you think, so you feel!

Reiki: Rei = wisdom & knowledge of the Universe
        Higher Intelligence that guides the creation +
        functioning of the Universe, wisdom that
        comes from God
    Ki: the life force that flows through everything

Healing: means "making whole" on all levels =
        mind, emotions + spirits as well as the body

Reiki helps clear blockages in a person's energy field.

Reiki healer

Healing:
○ Biomedical model - pills, injections
○ Holistic model - "wholistic" - whole person is treated - mind,
    emotions, spirits, environment, lifestyle - basis for folk
    cause - osteopathy, chiropractic, acupuncture + homeopathy
    aromatherapy, reflexology, spiritual healing Reiki
○ Metaphysical model: examines reality - everything is energy